Original title:

The Silent Dream

Author: Eliora Lumiste

ISBN HARDBACK: 978-9908-1-4648-5

ISBN PAPERBACK: 978-9908-1-4649-2

ISBN EBOOK: 978-9908-1-4650-8

The Quietude Between Heartbeats

In the stillness, whispers dwell,
Time suspended, secrets swell.
A moment's pause, the breath is sweet,
Life's rhythm slows, a sacred beat.

In shadowed corners, silence sings,
Unfolding dreams on gossamer wings.
Beyond the noise, a tranquil stream,
Where thoughts drift softly as a dream.

Reflections on a Clouded Mind

Thoughts like shadows, swirling fast,
Eclipsing moments, fading past.
A fog of doubt, a heavy shroud,
In depths unseen, I cry aloud.

Fragments glimmer, lost in haze,
Seeking clarity through the maze.
Each murmur trapped in tangled seams,
A search for solace, hope, and dreams.

Unseen Worlds Behind Closed Eyes

Within the depths of quiet night,
Imagination takes its flight.
Journeys far, where visions gleam,
Beyond the veil of waking dream.

Hidden realms where spirits play,
Colors dance and shadows sway.
A universe within my soul,
Where every heartbeat is made whole.

A Tapestry of Inaudible Longings

Threads of silence weave a song,
Yearnings deep where I belong.
Emotions linger, light as air,
In every heart, a whispered prayer.

Elusive hopes lie just beyond,
In the fabric of life, we're fond.
With every stitch, a tale unfolds,
Of dreams pursued and truths retold.

The Language of Night

Whispers in the shadows call,
Stars weave stories, silken thrall.
Moonlight dances, soft and bright,
Secrets shared in the still of night.

Dreams take flight on silent wings,
Echoes of forgotten things.
In the dark, hearts intertwine,
In the quiet, love can shine.

Serene Fantasies

Gentle waves kiss sandy shores,
Nature's lullabies, soft roars.
In the distance, mountains gleam,
A tapestry of whispered dream.

Clouds drift slowly, painted skies,
In this realm, true peace lies.
Mounting hope on azure tides,
In the heart, pure joy resides.

In the Heart of Silence

Stillness wraps the world around,
In the hush, lost dreams are found.
Time pauses, breath held tight,
In this space, thoughts take flight.

A gentle breeze becomes a song,
In this calm, we all belong.
Moments linger, softly sway,
In silence, we find our way.

Embracing the Unseen

Hands reach out to grasp the air,
To connect beyond the stare.
Invisible threads bind us tight,
Building bridges through the night.

Emotions dance in shades of gray,
Manifesting what words can't say.
In the quiet, truth reveals,
In the unseen, the heart heals.

Secrets of the Quiet Cosmos

Stars whisper softly, in the velvet night,
Planets spin slowly, in their endless flight.
Nebulas cradle, the dust of time,
Galaxies pulse softly, in a cosmic rhyme.

In shadows they linger, mysteries unfold,
Stories of stardust, whispered and told.
Lightyears traveling, from ages past,
Echoes of creation, in silence cast.

Celestial wonders, evoke silent dreams,
Infinity beckons, or so it seems.
A dance of existence, we blend and we sway,
In the quiet cosmos, where the lost find their way.

Traces of Forgotten Dreams

In twilight's glow, whispers softly fade,
Worn paths of memory, in shadows laid.
Fleeting visions drift, like leaves on the stream,
Resilient hope, still hints at the dream.

Echoes of laughter, in corners reside,
Ghosts of lost wishes, in silence abide.
Every heartbeat tells, tales long concealed,
Paths long abandoned, yet never repealed.

Underneath starlight, the past stirs alive,
Fleeting reflections, in stillness they thrive.
Each sigh and each tear, become part of the song,
Of traces unbroken, where we all belong.

Night's Gentle Breath

The moon softly glimmers, on a quilt of blue,
Embracing the silence, that whispers to you.
Stars blink in rhythm, like heartbeats slow,
In night's gentle breath, the world moves low.

Cool winds breathe softly, through branches high,
Crickets serenade, with a lullaby.
Dreams float like wishes, on clouds made of night,
Wrapped in the stillness, till dawn brings the light.

In shadows of comfort, we drift and we sway,
Cradled in silence, till the break of day.
Night whispers secrets, in soft, tender hues,
A moment of peace, where the heart can choose.

The Art of Silent Yearning

In corners of silence, our wishes abide,
Echoing softly, with nowhere to hide.
Yearning for moments, that slip through our hands,
Like grains of fine sand, on unmapped lands.

A gaze toward the horizon, dreams rise and fall,
In whispers unspoken, we hear the soft call.
Each heartbeat a canvas, where longing paints light,
A masterpiece woven, in the fabric of night.

In stillness we linger, with fragile desire,
Warm embers of hope, ignite hidden fire.
Through shadows we wander, uncharted, unseen,
Embracing the silence, where yearning convenes.

Quiet Light of the Mind

In the stillness of the night,
Thoughts flicker soft, like stars in flight.
A gentle glow begins to weave,
Shadows dance, as whispers cleave.

Memories drift on silver streams,
Carried forth by quiet dreams.
Tranquil moments, deeply sigh,
Illuminated, they never die.

Embers glow in twilight's grace,
Each reflection finds its place.
Softly glowing, thoughts align,
In this banquet, all is fine.

Voices linger, barely heard,
Echoes formed from every word.
In this silence, secrets dwell,
Quiet light, its magic cast so well.

As dawn breaks with tender brush,
The heart finds peace in every hush.
In the quiet, the mind shall soar,
Illuminated evermore.

The Art of Unvoiced Desires

In the shadows of the heart,
Yearnings play a hidden part.
Whispers soft, like petals fall,
Artistry in silence, after all.

In the quiet, dreams take flight,
Crafted hues in soft twilight.
Unspoken words, a canvas bare,
Desires bloom without a care.

Gentle stars in velvet skies,
Illuminate the truth in sighs.
Every glance holds tales untold,
In the silence, passions bold.

Brush of longing paints the night,
In the dark, hopes burn so bright.
The art of love, both still and deep,
Awake in hearts that dare to keep.

From silence, blossoms rise anew,
Crafted dreams in every hue.
Unvoiced desires find their way,
In the quiet, forever stay.

Serenity's Hidden Path

In quiet glades where whispers tread,
Footsteps softly, dreams are fed.
By the brook, the breezes weave,
Serenity grants what we believe.

Pathways twist through dappled light,
Guiding souls through day and night.
Every step, a gentle prayer,
Finding peace in tender air.

Mossy stones and ancient trees,
Cradle thoughts on wandering breeze.
Underneath the vaulted sky,
A hidden path, where spirits fly.

Echoes linger in the green,
Nature's grace, a sacred scene.
In stillness, hearts begin to sing,
The joy that every moment brings.

Serenity flows through every curve,
In wonder, we find the nerve.
To walk the path where dreams arise,
In quietude, our spirits rise.

Songs of a Hushed Heart

Deep within, a quiet tune,
Lingers softly, like a moon.
Hushed emotions softly play,
A melody that finds its way.

Gentle echoes in the night,
Cradle dreams with soft delight.
Each heartbeat whispers, light as air,
In this stillness, love lays bare.

Unheard symphonies unfold,
In the depths, where stories told.
Every sigh, a note divine,
Songs composed in hearts that pine.

Moments pass, yet softly cling,
In the silence, praises sing.
A hushed heart finds its song of grace,
In the quiet, a sacred space.

With every chord, the shadows dance,
Tracing paths of sweet romance.
In the calm, the heart will find,
The beauty of a love entwined.

Tides of Calm Reflection

Gentle waves caress the shore,
Soft whispers of the ocean's lore.
Time stands still, a quiet grace,
In nature's arms, we find our place.

Moonlight dances on the sea,
Shimmering paths of tranquility.
Each breath taken, a soothing sound,
In this peace, our hearts are found.

The horizon blushes with the dawn,
Awakening hopes, a new day drawn.
In stillness, dreams begin to rise,
Bathed in golden morning skies.

Ripples bring tales of old,
Secrets of the deep, softly told.
In reflection, we lose and find,
The forgotten layers of our mind.

As daylight fades into the night,
We hold our wishes, burning bright.
In the calm, we learn to see,
The tides that flow, and set us free.

Whispered Secrets of the Soul

In quiet corners, shadows play,
Softly guiding words we say.
The heart speaks slowly, a tender tune,
Under the watchful gaze of the moon.

The whispers echo through the trees,
Carried gently by the breeze.
Each secret murmured, a treasured thread,
Woven in silence, where fears are shed.

In the stillness, truths arise,
Reflections caught in starlit skies.
We find the strength to bare our core,
To share the stories never told before.

Through storms of doubt, we learn to fly,
With whispered hopes that never die.
In the shadows, we grasp the light,
Illuminating paths, bold and bright.

Bound by whispers, we unite,
In every sorrow, in every flight.
The soul's soft secrets entwined in grace,
Together we find our sacred space.

The Silent Canvas of Night

Stars paint stories in the dark,
Every twinkle, a fleeting spark.
The moon hangs high, a watchful gaze,
Guiding dreams through twilight haze.

Soft shadows dance on quiet ground,
Where the lost and found are gently bound.
In stillness, serenity unfolds,
As a masterpiece of silence molds.

Whispers of night breathe deep and slow,
Carrying secrets only they know.
In the calm, the world recedes,
Nurturing the heart's quiet needs.

Painted skies, a velvet cloak,
Where the night unfolds, dreams are spoke.
In the quiet, the soul finds peace,
In the boundless night, all worries cease.

With each heartbeat, the canvas grows,
Draped in stars, the night bestows.
In silence, we find our flight,
On the silent canvas of the night.

Beneath the Veil of Solitude

In shadows deep where whispers dwell,
A silent heart begins to swell.
Lost dreams float like autumn leaves,
Entwined in webs the silence weaves.

Beneath the stars, the night does sigh,
With every breath, a fleeting lie.
The echoes haunt the hollow space,
In solitude, I find my grace.

Time drips slow like melting wax,
In solitude, my spirit asks.
For solace found in quiet's fold,
A secret kept, yet to be told.

The moonlit path, it beckons near,
Each step I take, I face my fear.
In stillness, I confront the truth,
The beauty wrapped in fragile youth.

Through velvet nights, the heart beats strong,
In solitude, I find my song.
A melody of soft despair,
Beneath the veil, I breathe the air.

Echoes of Yesteryears

In dusty tomes of faded dreams,
The past resounds in whispered themes.
Each page a canvas worn and old,
Of stories lost and tales retold.

Through moments trapped in time's embrace,
I wander through a spectral space.
With echoes dancing on the wind,
The threads of life begin to blend.

Pictures framed in golden hue,
Hold fragments of a life I knew.
The laughter rings, though voices fade,
In shadows where the light betrayed.

Beneath the oak, where memories lay,
I chase the ghosts of yesterday.
Their whispers tickle at my ear,
A haunting song I long to hear.

Yet in the echoes, hope remains,
A tapestry of joys and pains.
For through the storms of fleeting years,
I find my strength beyond the tears.

A Symphony of Unspoken Words

In starlit nights where silence sings,
The heart, it knows what music brings.
A symphony of thoughts untamed,
In every glance, a feeling framed.

With every heartbeat, stories spin,
In unvoiced dreams, we dare begin.
Expressions dance upon the air,
In quiet realms, our souls lay bare.

A gentle touch, a fleeting smile,
Each moment lived, an endless mile.
Through whispered hopes and muted sighs,
The language spoken through our eyes.

In twilight's glow, emotions rise,
A melody, where silence lies.
The beauty found in what we hide,
In every breath, our hearts confide.

Thus let the world in silence hear,
The symphony we hold so dear.
For in the stillness, dreams unfurl,
A dance of love that spins the world.

In the Cradle of Night

As shadows curl and daylight fades,
The night unveils its silk cascades.
In quiet corners, secrets hold,
A tapestry of stories told.

Beneath the watchful, silver moon,
The stars confess their quiet tunes.
Each glimmer holds a whispered wish,
A moment sealed, a fleeting bliss.

In midnight's arms, the heart finds peace,
As worries melt, the burdens cease.
With every breath, the silence sighs,
In this embrace, the spirit flies.

As dreams take flight on velvet wings,
I wander through what nighttime brings.
Each thought a world, a vast expanse,
In the cradle of night, I dance.

So let the dawn keep still its chase,
For here I find my sacred space.
In shadows deep, I carve my light,
Forever wrapped in love's delight.

Dreams Wrapped in Stillness

In twilight's gentle embrace,
Silent whispers softly trace.
Eyes closed tight, worlds collide,
In the stillness, dreams abide.

Stars unveil their secret glow,
Guiding paths where spirits flow.
Night unfolds its velvet skies,
Cradling hope where magic lies.

Each breath a tender sigh,
As shadows drift and softly fly.
Thoughts dance lightly, free and bold,
In silence, stories are told.

Embraced by night's deep grace,
Finding solace in this space.
With hearts entwined, we wander free,
In stillness, just you and me.

Awake within a dream's refrain,
A timeless bond, a sweet domain.
Here, in quiet, we reside,
In the haven of the night's glide.

Brushed by Sleep's Caress

With each flutter of the eye,
The world fades, a soft goodbye.
Gentle breath, a rhythmic ease,
In this moment, I find peace.

Sleep whispers low, a tender call,
Wrapping warmth, it holds us all.
Each shadow blends, and time stands still,
In dreams, we drift, our hearts to fill.

Floating on a silver breeze,
Lost in echoes, sweet reprise.
The night sings softly, velvety tune,
Cradling us beneath the moon.

Every sigh a lullaby,
As we voyage through the sky.
Held by night, we're far apart,
Yet closer still, heart to heart.

Awake, the dawn begins to rise,
Yet still, we linger, soft goodbyes.
Brushed by sleep, in dreams we trust,
In daylight's touch, our spirits rust.

Beyond the Reach of Sound

In silence spun, the night unfolds,
A tapestry of stories told.
Quiet echoes dance through time,
In spaces vast, soft rhythms chime.

Stars align in cosmic grace,
Whispers linger, soft embrace.
Beyond the noise, where dreams reside,
Boundless love, our hearts confide.

Each moment swells, a breath of air,
In gentle night, we drift and share.
Thoughts unspoken, feelings pure,
In tranquil depths, we find our cure.

Here, where silence finds its voice,
In darkness deep, we make our choice.
To dance with shadows, lover's guide,
Beyond the reach, where dreams abide.

So let us wander, hand in hand,
In silence deep, a promised land.
Beyond the reach of sound and sight,
Together lost, within the night.

Whispers Beneath the Stars

Underneath the vast, dark sky,
The stars twinkle, oh so high.
Softly, dreams begin to weave,
In silent moments, we believe.

Rustling leaves, a calming breath,
In nature's arms, we find our depth.
Whispers sent on midnight air,
Carried forth without a care.

Moonlight spills in gentle streams,
Bathing us in silver dreams.
Echoes of a tender tune,
Filling hearts beneath the moon.

In shadows deep, our secrets lay,
Where wishes dance, and spirits play.
Hand in hand, we chase the night,
Whispers, soft, in pure delight.

Here we pause, beneath the glow,
As the softest breezes blow.
With every star, a wish we cast,
In whispers shared, our bond will last.

Solitude's Soft Embrace

In twilight's hush, I find my calm,
Whispers of night, a soothing balm.
Stars gently blink in the vast expanse,
In solitude's arms, I take my chance.

Thoughts like shadows drift in the night,
Wrapped in silence, I feel the light.
Each breath a moment, a pause, a sigh,
In solitude's soft embrace, I fly.

Emotions weave like threads of gold,
Stories of dreams and tales untold.
A world of peace within my heart,
In solitude, I find my art.

The moonlight dances upon the sea,
Reflecting hopes and memories.
With every wave that kisses the shore,
I embrace the stillness, I crave for more.

And as the dawn begins to break,
I know the day will softly wake.
Yet in the quiet, I always find,
Solitude's love, forever kind.

Chasing Shadows of Tomorrow

In the dusk, where whispers dwell,
I chase the dreams that time won't tell.
Through the alleys of the unknown,
I seek the light, but walk alone.

Shadows flicker in the fading light,
Guiding paths through the velvet night.
Each corner hides a secret thought,
In chasing shadows, battles fought.

Tomorrow's promise lingers near,
But hope and doubt, they intertwine here.
With every step, a choice I make,
From darkened paths, I will awake.

The stars above my heart ignite,
A beacon call in the deep of night.
In every flicker lies a song,
Chasing shadows where I belong.

And when the dawn begins its song,
I'll find the place where I am strong.
In chasing dreams, I hear the sound,
That tomorrow's light will soon be found.

The Realm of Unsung Wishes

In whispers soft, dreams start to bloom,
In hidden corners, dispelling gloom.
Each wish a star in the nighttime sky,
In the realm of hope, they linger high.

With every heartbeat, a longing grows,
Silent affirmations, the heart bestows.
In shadows deep, where echoes play,
Unsung wishes find their way.

Moments float like leaves on streams,
Carried away, but not the dreams.
A silent prayer, a whispered sigh,
In this realm of wishes, we dare to fly.

Through endless nights and shining days,
I chase the light in myriad ways.
For every thought that dares to rise,
In the realm of wishes, hope never dies.

And when the world feels heavy and cold,
I seek the stories yet to be told.
For in this realm, my heart takes flight,
In the realm of unsung wishes, I find my light.

Nocturnal Echoes

The night unfolds its quiet grace,
In shadows deep, we find our place.
Echoes linger, soft and clear,
In nocturnal whispers, we disappear.

Stars above like diamonds shine,
In the stillness, hearts intertwine.
Fleeting moments, hushed and slow,
Nocturnal echoes, a tender glow.

With every breath, the night unveils,
Secrets woven in soft veils.
A symphony of dreams takes flight,
In nocturnal echoes, we unite.

Through silver paths, the moonlight drapes,
Quiet tales of forgotten shapes.
A dance of loss, a song of grace,
In the night's embrace, we find our space.

As dawn approaches, soft and bright,
We hold the echoes of the night.
For every whisper, every sigh,
In nocturnal echoes, we learn to fly.

A Canvas of Quiet Longing

In twilight's glow, the silence weaves,
Colors of dreams that the heart believes.
Brush strokes of hope on a canvas bare,
Whispers of wishes dance in the air.

Shadows of yearning softly unfold,
Stories untold by the night's gentle hold.
Each heartbeat echoes through the still,
A masterpiece born of desire and will.

With every sigh, the canvas expands,
Painting the future with fragile hands.
Moments of longing, tender and true,
Awaiting the dawn wrapped in hues of blue.

A tapestry woven with threads of time,
Silent confessions in rhythm and rhyme.
Dreams take flight on the wings of night,
A canvas alive with the softest light.

Sleep's Tender Promises

In shadows deep, where worries fade,
Sleep weaves a quilt, a gentle cascade.
Cradled in dreams, the spirit takes flight,
Wrapped in the warmth of the velvet night.

Whispers of peace serenade the soul,
Filling the heart with a tranquil role.
Stars twinkle softly, a lullaby's call,
In the arms of slumber, we surrender all.

The world outside fades into the mist,
In sleep's embrace, there's naught to resist.
Tender promises from distant skies,
Allowing us solace as daylight dies.

A journey unfolds as our eyes softly close,
Amidst the night, where serenity flows.
Each breath a lull, a rhythmic sigh,
Carrying dreams where our spirits fly.

Unspoken Journeys

In the quiet mind, a map appears,
Paths unexplored through laughter and tears.
Softly we wander where silence reigns,
A melody plays where the heart contains.

Each step a heartbeat in the dark unknown,
A whispered promise, we're never alone.
Through valleys of doubt and mountains of hope,
We travel the lines of our joy and scope.

Guided by stars that illuminate dreams,
Navigating life through uncharted streams.
With courage in hand, we embrace the night,
Venturing forth, seeking endless light.

Written in shadows, the stories unfold,
Of journeys unspoken, both timid and bold.
An odyssey woven through the threads of time,
In echoes of silence, life's rhythm and rhyme.

Where Stillness Breathes

In the hush of dawn, where stillness breathes,
Nature unfolds as the world believes.
Gentle whispers brush against the trees,
A symphony played by the waking breeze.

Mountains stand guard in the soft morning light,
Cradling secrets as day chases night.
The river flows calm, a reflective sigh,
Mirroring dreams as the moments fly.

Every leaf dances in a timeless sway,
Echoing harmony woven in gray.
In stillness, we find what the heart cannot say,
A sanctuary gathered where shadows play.

Here in this space, our spirits align,
United with nature, both gentle and divine.
In quietude, hope takes its sacred place,
Where stillness breathes, we find our grace.

Silent Footsteps on Dreamscapes

In shadows soft, they tread so light,
Whispers weave through the quiet night.
Where visions dance on shimmering beams,
Silent footsteps glide through dreams.

Stars above, they softly gaze,
Lost in the ethereal haze.
Each step a thread, a tale to tell,
In a world where wishes dwell.

Gentle winds call out their name,
Echoes flicker like a flame.
Guided by hope, they drift and soar,
In this land forevermore.

The moonlight kisses the soft ground,
In this silence, peace is found.
Footprints fade as new dreams rise,
Carried high on starlit skies.

Through valleys deep, and mountains tall,
The echoes of dreams in twilight call.
With each heartbeat, they come alive,
In the realm where spirits thrive.

The Stillness of Being

In a moment, the world stands still,
Time suspended, a gentle thrill.
Whispers linger in serene air,
A tranquil pulse, releasing care.

The heart knows peace, a silent song,
In this calm where we belong.
Each breath a wave, soft and slow,
Embracing stillness, letting go.

Beneath the stars, shimmering bright,
Awakens a sense of pure light.
In shadows deep, we find our way,
In the stillness, we choose to stay.

Every sigh a gentle breeze,
Rustling leaves in quiet trees.
Harmony flows through every vein,
In silence, all is gained.

The world outside may rush and race,
But in this stillness, we find grace.
Moments captured, softly seized,
In the stillness, hearts are eased.

Guided by Unseen Hands

In the dark, a touch so light,
Fingers beckon through the night.
Whispers flow like silver streams,
Guided softly by unseen dreams.

Paths unfold beneath our feet,
Echoes of a heartbeat's beat.
With each twist, a gentle pull,
Navigating where hearts are full.

A tapestry of distant stars,
Threads of fate from afar.
Though the way may twist and bend,
We walk on faith, our unseen friend.

Through trials that seem far too grand,
We stand tall, held by these hands.
Trust in the guidance, fierce and true,
Each step leading us to renew.

Invisible threads weave through our days,
Binding destinies in mystic ways.
In the silence, they leave their mark,
Sparking light within the dark.

In Search of Lost Whispers

In the hush of twilight's song,
We wander where we feel we belong.
Seeking echoes of days gone by,
Where memories linger and never die.

Whispers carried on the breeze,
Softly weaving through ancient trees.
In shadows cast by fading light,
We chase the dreams that take to flight.

Each breath reveals a story told,
In visions bright, both new and old.
Lost in the mists, we search and roam,
In these whispers, we find our home.

Faint voices murmur a sacred tune,
Under the watchful eye of the moon.
Through tangled paths, we deftly glide,
With faith as our compass, we decide.

The heart remembers what time can't erase,
Each whisper a trace of a cherished place.
In the silence, we bring to light,
The lost whispers that feel so right.

Shadows of Unspoken Visions

In the depth of night, they linger slow,
Whispers carried by the wind's soft flow.
Silhouettes dance in the fading light,
Casting dreams as stars ignite.

Each shadow speaks in silent grace,
Echoes found in a hidden place.
Fragments of hope in dark's embrace,
Unseen truths we all must face.

The moon reveals what eyes can't see,
A tapestry of what could be.
In the stillness, visions roam,
Guiding hearts that seek a home.

Fleeting moments, a chance to sigh,
Comfort found in the night sky.
As shadows weave their intricate seams,
We awaken to our deepest dreams.

With every breath, the night unfolds,
Stories waiting to be told.
In between the black and white,
Shadows dance, embracing light.

Hushed Reveries in Twilight

In twilight's glow, the world holds breath,
A gentle pause between life and death.
Dreams entwined with fading day,
Hushed whispers in the soft decay.

Colors blend in a soft embrace,
As shadows chase the sun's last trace.
Silence sings a tender tune,
While stars awaken, one by one.

With open hearts, we watch and wait,
For twilight's charm to captivate.
Each moment woven in its spell,
Lifts our spirits, ours to tell.

The tranquil sigh of the evening breeze,
Carries dreams with effortless ease.
In the hush, our souls take flight,
Finding solace in the night.

As darkness drapes the earth anew,
We find the strength in shadows too.
Hushed reveries become our guide,
In twilight's arms, we gently bide.

Veils of the Unseen

Beneath the veil, the secrets dwell,
Stories woven from an ancient spell.
Hidden paths in shadows tight,
Whispers beckon in the night.

What lies beneath the surface gray?
Wonders waiting in the sway.
Eyes that search for the hidden true,
Finding beauty in the blue.

Life unfolds in a muted hue,
Veils of meaning shifting through.
Gentle nudges, a quiet hand,
Guide us softly to understand.

In the depths, the echoes sway,
Shaping thoughts that play all day.
A dance of fleeting, unseen dreams,
Life is more than what it seems.

As time reveals each tender line,
Truth emerges from divine design.
In veils of dusk, our hearts take flight,
Embracing all that feels so right.

Serenity's Unheard Ballad

In stillness, where the rivers flow,
A ballad hums, soft and low.
Nature's chorus cradles time,
Whispers sweet in rhythm and rhyme.

Beneath the trees, a quiet song,
Serenity sings, gentle and strong.
Each note a touch from the hand of fate,
Guiding hearts to contemplate.

With open ears, we learn to feel,
The magic of what's truly real.
In shadows deep, the echoes sway,
Serenity leads us on our way.

As dawn breaks with a golden hue,
Melodies of peace are born anew.
Unheard ballads in the dawn's embrace,
Invite our souls to find their place.

In every moment spent in grace,
The unheard waits in a sacred space.
Embraced by nature's timeless theme,
We find ourselves within the dream.

A Solitary Canvas

Upon the shore of quiet dreams,
A blank space waits for whispered themes.
Waves of thought beside the sand,
Brush strokes flicker, life unplanned.

Colors mix in sunset's glow,
Each hue a story yet to show.
With every stroke, the heart takes flight,
Transforming darkness into light.

Loneliness paints its soft embrace,
Each line revealing hidden grace.
In solitude, true art is born,
A masterpiece from stillness worn.

In every shadow, every trace,
Life finds a way to leave its space.
The canvas waits, its whispers clear,
Art emerges from quiet fear.

The artist stands, a fleeting soul,
Creating beauty, making whole.
In solitude, the colors sing,
A heart released, it learns to wing.

Celestial Soliloquy

Stars align in silent realms,
Whispers echo, thoughts it helms.
Constellations hold their breath,
In the night, a dance with death.

Planets spin in gentle grace,
Galaxies in a timeless race.
Each twinkle tells a tale untold,
The universe, an age-old mold.

Moonlight bathes the world in dreams,
Softly spilling silver beams.
Hearts converse with cosmic sway,
In this vast, celestial play.

Nebulas of vibrant hue,
Crafting skies of endless blue.
In silence, worlds collide and fade,
A soliloquy unafraid.

Among the stars, a truth we find,
A glimpse of heart, a glimpse of mind.
In cosmic dance, we weave our fate,
In stardust, love transcends the weight.

The Quiet Between Heartbeats

In a moment, time does pause,
A heartbeat whispers soft applause.
Between the ticks of life's refrain,
Silence finds its sacred gain.

Breath held tight, anxiety fades,
In stillness, truth gently wades.
A heartbeat's rhythm, soft and slow,
Echoes in the calm we know.

Feeling sways in silent space,
Time lingers, etched in grace.
A sigh escapes, a fleeting sound,
In the quiet, life is found.

Hands connect and souls seek peace,
In silence, whispers seem to cease.
Every heartbeat tells a tale,
In tranquil moments where we sail.

Love, a pulse, a sacred dance,
In the stillness, hearts take chance.
Between the beats, true life abounds,
In quietude, our essence grounds.

Dreamscapes in the Twilight

In twilight's glow, the world transforms,
Daylight wanes, as silence warms.
Thoughts wander through the dusky haze,
Lost in wistful, hazy ways.

Shadows stretch, the colors bleed,
Cascading dreams from every deed.
Laughter lingers, soft and sweet,
In this realm where spirits meet.

Stars awaken, the night unfolds,
Echoes of stories yet untold.
Each whisper paints a vivid scene,
In the air, a magic sheen.

Across horizons, horizons blend,
In twilight, beginnings never end.
Dreams take flight on sleepy wings,
In dusk, the heart finds what it sings.

Reflections of the day reside,
In twilight's arms, they safely hide.
Every moment, a fleeting flight,
In dreamscapes bathed in soft twilight.

Dreams Carved in Soft Silence

In twilight's hush, we weave our dreams,
A tapestry of gentle seams.
Whispers float on starlit air,
In soft silence, we lay bare.

Stars blink softly, secrets unfold,
Stories of the brave and bold.
In shadows cast by moon's embrace,
We find our hopes, a sacred space.

Silhouettes dance on velvet night,
A chorus of souls taking flight.
With every breath, the silence sighs,
As dreams awaken, touching skies.

Embers glow in the quiet deep,
In the stillness, our hearts leap.
Each wish a star, each heartbeat a wave,
In soft silence, we become brave.

So let the night our secrets keep,
In dreams where silence runs so deep.
Together, in this sacred refrain,
We carve our dreams, and love remains.

A Symphony of Distant Whispers

In the distance, whispers call,
A symphony for one and all.
Moonlit paths where shadows sway,
Echoes of the night and day.

Fragrant blooms in breezy dance,
Softly beckon, give us a chance.
In every rustle, in every sigh,
We hear the world's sweet lullaby.

Every corner holds a song,
In this place where we belong.
With each whisper, a soul ignites,
Binding hearts on starry nights.

Notes of laughter, tears of grace,
Time and space begin to chase.
In this symphony, love accords,
A harmony that never wards.

So let the whispers gently weave,
A tapestry that we believe.
In the silence, hear the tune,
A symphony beneath the moon.

Unvoiced Journeys in the Dark

In shadows thick, our spirits roam,
Unvoiced journeys lead us home.
With every step, our hearts take flight,
We wander softly through the night.

Paths untraveled, dreams unheard,
In silence, we find the spoken word.
Each twist and turn a tale unfolds,
In the dark, our truth behold.

Stars above like lanterns gleam,
Guiding us through night's soft dream.
Though words remain forever lost,
Our hearts, they know the worth, the cost.

Each moment wrapped in sweet refrain,
Our souls connected, love's domain.
In the stillness, journeys blend,
Unvoiced whispers never end.

So as we walk this hidden path,
In every silence, feel the bath.
For in the dark, our spirits spark,
Unvoiced journeys leave their mark.

Beneath the Cloak of Night

Beneath the cloak of velvet night,
The world begins to dim its light.
Stars emerge, like diamonds rare,
In the stillness, we lay bare.

Moonlight spills on whispered dreams,
In darkness, hope brightly beams.
With every breath, the shadows blend,
In night's embrace, we find a friend.

The owls call from branches high,
As silver clouds drift slowly by.
Each heartbeat echoes in the dark,
Igniting fires, igniting spark.

Paths revealed in gleaming glow,
In silence deep, our spirits flow.
Under the cloak, our fears take flight,
Dancing softly in the night.

So let us wander hand in hand,
Through the dreams, through shadows grand.
Beneath the cloak, our souls take flight,
In the embrace of soft, sweet night.

In the Shadow of Light

In whispers the dawn begins to break,
Soft beams unfurl where shadows awake.
The world held its breath, in hushed delight,
A dance of colors ignites the night.

Fleeting glances of gold on the stream,
Mirrors of hope, like a waking dream.
Each moment a spark in a vast embrace,
In the shadow of light, we find our place.

Tender breaths of a morning's sigh,
Inviting the warmth as the stars pass by.
Chasing the echoes of what haunts the deep,
In the shadow of light, our secrets keep.

A gentle caress from the sun's sweet rays,
Guiding lost spirits through a sunlit maze.
Reflection of life in the fluttering leaves,
In the shadow of light, our heart believes.

As dusk descends on the amber sky,
A promise lingers, a soft goodbye.
Nightfall wraps all in its velvet flight,
We linger forever in the shadow of light.

To Dance in the Quiet

In still air where thoughts freely sway,
Whispers and echoes quietly play.
Each moment unfolds, a gentle embrace,
To dance in the quiet, find our grace.

The moon weaves its silver across the night,
Stars twinkle softly, gifted with light.
In shadows we sway, under velvet skies,
To dance in the quiet, where magic lies.

Beneath the soft rustle of leaves up high,
We hear the sweet hush of a lullaby.
In secret alcoves, dreams take flight,
To dance in the quiet, hearts burn bright.

Subtle are steps where the soft winds blow,
Guiding our souls in a rhythmic flow.
Where silence reigns and whispers ignite,
To dance in the quiet, spirits in flight.

As twilight blooms in a tapestry spun,
We find our rhythm, two hearts as one.
In the hush of the night, pure love ignites,
To dance in the quiet, lost in the light.

Visions Shrouded in Stillness

In corners of dreams where silence is deep,
Visions awaken from shadows they keep.
A tapestry woven of whispers and sighs,
Visions shrouded in stillness, calm as the skies.

The world spins softly on its ancient wheel,
Moments suspended, what do we feel?
Thoughts drift like petals on water's face,
Visions shrouded in stillness, time finds its grace.

A fragrance of memories lingers on air,
Carried in twilight, they whisper and share.
Softly they beckon, like stars shining bright,
Visions shrouded in stillness, lost in the night.

When chaos retreats, and peace finds its way,
In the cradle of dusk, our hearts gently sway.
Through valleys of shadows, lost dreams take flight,
Visions shrouded in stillness, bathed in soft light.

In echoes of longing, our souls intertwine,
In silence we gather, through moments divine.
For in every heartbeat, there lies the insight,
Visions shrouded in stillness, forever in sight.

Reveries of the Unseen

In the hush of the night, dreams softly bloom,
Reveries beckon, dispelling the gloom.
Quietly woven in mystical thread,
Reveries of the unseen, where spirits are fed.

Moonlight dances on the edges of thought,
Casting shadows of wonders, tenderly sought.
Where hope flutters gently, and fears are laid bare,
Reveries of the unseen float softly in the air.

In gardens of silence, where echoes find grace,
Petals of wisdom adorn every space.
Whispers of longing in twilight's embrace,
Reveries of the unseen, a timeless chase.

With eyes closed to daylight, we wander along,
In realms of the heart, we discover our song.
Each secret a thread in the fabric of dreams,
Reveries of the unseen unravel their themes.

As dawn breaks anew and shadows retreat,
The treasures of night make our journey complete.
In the light of the morn, we'll carry the scene,
Reveries of the unseen, forever serene.

An Invitation to Stillness

In whispers of the evening air,
The world slows down, a gentle snare.
Find peace beneath the twilight's glow,
Where time and thought begin to flow.

Close your eyes and breathe it in,
Let thoughts dissolve, let calm begin.
The heart finds solace in the night,
Embracing shadows, seeking light.

The stars unveil a silent song,
A melody where you belong.
Stillness beckons, soft and clear,
Inviting you to linger near.

Each moment stretches, softly drawn,
Beneath the watchful gaze of dawn.
In quietude, your spirit flies,
As consciousness begins to rise.

So heed the call, and take a seat,
In stillness, find the world complete.
An invitation to the soul,
To grasp the whole in fragments small.

The Unseen Horizon

Beyond the peaks, where skies do meet,
Lies a horizon, bittersweet.
The sun dips low, a painter's brush,
In colors bold, in shadows hush.

With every step, a journey lies,
In whispered dreams and hopeful sighs.
The path unfolds, though eyes can't see,
A promise waits, a destiny.

In wandering hearts, a spark ignites,
Curiosity fuels the nights.
Each star a guide, each breeze a friend,
Leading us forth, onward, ascend.

The unseen calls, a siren's song,
To trust the journey, where we belong.
Beyond the veil of what we know,
Beckons the dawn with each new glow.

So chase the light and shed your fears,
Embrace the dreams, and keep them near.
The unseen horizon holds the key,
Unlocking all that we can be.

Shadows Speak in Silence

In corners dark, where whispers creep,
The shadows gather secrets deep.
They weave a tale of days long past,
In quietude, their voices cast.

With every flicker of the flame,
They cling to memories, speak a name.
In silence, stories come alive,
Where echoes dance and spirits thrive.

They share the weight of time's embrace,
A gentle touch, a haunting grace.
In twilight hours, their murmurs blend,
A tapestry of hearts to mend.

So lend an ear to sounds unseen,
In twilight's glow, where shadows glean.
For in their depths, the truth resides,
A symphony where hope abides.

The shadows speak, though soft and low,
Of dreams fulfilled and lost in woe.
In silence carved, their voices rise,
Revealing worlds beyond the skies.

The Weight of Unsung Melodies

In quiet rooms where echoes dwell,
The weight of music, hard to tell.
Melodies linger, soft and light,
In hearts like shadows, out of sight.

Each note a whisper, a fleeting dream,
Unheard by many, yet they seem
To pulse with life, a hidden song,
Carrying feelings, deep and strong.

In silence, the unsung notes will play,
Of love and loss, of night and day.
They linger on the edge of thought,
A private language, dearly sought.

Those notes unplayed, the voices shy,
Bear tales of longing, drifting by.
Through silent cries and secret hopes,
In melodies, our spirit copes.

So listen close to the air around,
For unsung songs, in silence found.
The weight they carry, pure and true,
Beckons the heart to dance anew.

The Stillness of Gossamer Thoughts

In silence wrapped, the whispers blend,
Soft echoes rise where reflections wend.
A gentle breeze through twilight's glance,
Carrying dreams in a fragile trance.

Veils of thought, like threads of light,
Glimmer softly in the night.
Each moment held, a fleeting grace,
In stillness found, a sacred space.

Time unravels, a tapestry wide,
Colors merge, like waves that slide.
In gentle hums, the heart takes flight,
To dance with shadows, lost from sight.

Wisps of hope among the stars,
Whirling softly, beyond our scars.
In quietude, we find our voice,
In every thought, a hidden choice.

Beneath the surface, life unfurls,
In gossamer threads, the dreamer swirls.
A world unseen, yet deeply felt,
In stillness, where our hearts are knelt.

Lullabies of an Absent Mind

In soft shadows where memories lay,
Drifting echoes of a fading day.
A gentle hum, the silence sings,
Wrapped in thoughts like fragile wings.

The clock ticks on, a measured dance,
Time evades, slips through chance.
In reverie, the heart finds peace,
In wandering dreams, a sweet release.

Clouds of wonder, draped in mist,
Kisses of night, a tender tryst.
Cradled thoughts in a fleeting sigh,
Where whispers linger and hopes lie.

A lullaby for quiet minds,
Where lost treasures the spirit finds.
In every note, a heartbeat's song,
In absent dreams, we still belong.

As stars align with gentle grace,
We find our light in this hidden space.
A tapestry of thoughts unwind,
Lullabies soft, forever bind.

Fantasies Adrift in Still Waters

Beneath the calm, where secrets dwell,
Fleeting dreams weave their silent spell.
Rippling reflections in moonlit gleam,
Waves of quiet, the heart's soft stream.

Ebbing tides of thoughts so rare,
Drifting softly, void of care.
Each fantasy, a ship's embrace,
Sailing under a starry lace.

In shallow depths, where wonders blend,
Currents carry, they gently send.
Hopeful hearts on waters vast,
Seeking solace, forgetting the past.

For every wave a tale unfolds,
Of distant shores and treasures untold.
In stillness, dreams are drawn anew,
In quiet depths, the spirit grew.

Fantasies float on gentle streams,
In whispered waters, we find our dreams.
A world created, serene and bright,
Adrift in stillness, on through the night.

Starlit Paths of Unuttered Wishes

On velvet nights, where silence roams,
Starlit paths lead our wandering homes.
With whispered hopes upon the air,
We trace the light, find solace there.

Each twinkling star, a wish concealed,
A map of dreams long unrevealed.
In cosmic dance, our spirits blend,
On paths where lost desires mend.

Carried forth on celestial wings,
The heart remembers what longing brings.
In shadows cast by endless skies,
Unuttered wishes, where magic lies.

A melody plays on nights so clear,
The universe speaks, if we dare hear.
In every twinkle, a story told,
Of journeys taken, of hearts so bold.

In stillness found beneath the night,
We grasp the sparks, ignite the light.
With starlit paths, we dance and sway,
Guided by dreams that won't fade away.

Whispers of Fate

In the silence of night, secrets entwine,
Fates dance like shadows, so softly divine.
Paths that we tread, woven with care,
A tapestry rich, spun in the air.

Whispers of time, calling our names,
Echoes of choices, bright as the flames.
Moments that linger, float like a sigh,
Guiding our hearts like stars in the sky.

In the depth of the dark, hope softly glows,
Carried on breezes where destiny flows.
Silent decisions etched in the mind,
Every small step, a treasure to find.

Threads in the fabric, unseen yet so real,
Fingers of fate, we tentatively feel.
Bound by our dreams, we wander and roam,
Chasing the echoes that lead us back home.

With each passing heartbeat, we learn to embrace,
The whispers of fate, in the quietest space.
A journey of trust, through shadows and light,
Guided by whispers that bloom in the night.

Echoes in Stillness

In the stillness of dawn, echoes resound,
Whispers of morning, softly abound.
Gentle reminders of dreams left behind,
Carried on breezes, elusive and kind.

Calm waters reflect the sky's soft embrace,
Moments of silence can pause time and space.
Nature's soft murmurs, a tranquil refrain,
Calling our spirits to dance in the rain.

As shadows retreat, the light gently plays,
Painting the world in a golden haze.
Each heartbeat aligns with the rhythm of day,
In echoes of stillness, we drift and sway.

The pulse of the earth, a song of its own,
In whispers and sighs, our hearts have grown.
Lost in the beauty of all that we see,
In echoes of stillness, just you and me.

With each fleeting moment, the world starts to breathe,
In the canvas of quiet, we learn to believe.
Echoes of stillness, a balm to the soul,
Binding together, we find ourselves whole.

A Lullaby for Shadows

In the cradle of night, shadows take flight,
Weaving soft dreams, hidden from sight.
A lullaby whispers, sweet and sincere,
Gentle as moonbeams, calming all fear.

Sleepy-eyed wanderers drift through their fears,
Guided by starlight, washed in their tears.
A melody dances on the night's breath,
A lullaby soothing, embracing our depth.

In the heart of the dark, solace we find,
In shadows of memories, both gentle and kind.
The hush of the night, a promise so pure,
In a lullaby's arms, we feel safe and sure.

Soft whispers gather, like blankets of night,
Cradling our dreams, making everything right.
Every lost moment finds home, every sigh,
A lullaby sung, as the stars softly die.

So let go of worries, let the shadows play,
In the stillness of night, they'll lead us away.
With a lullaby's grace, we drift on the wind,
Embraced by the shadows, where journeys begin.

Murmurs of the Moonlit Mind

In the glow of the moon, thoughts softly churn,
Murmurs of wisdom, enticingly burn.
Ideas take flight on wings of the night,
In the stillness of dreams, they shimmer and light.

Through the fabric of darkness, secrets arise,
Wrapped in the glow of the starlit skies.
A symphony played on the strings of our soul,
Murmurs that guide us, making us whole.

With each gentle breeze, the whispers grow clear,
Carried by time, they draw ever near.
Exploring the depths of the mind's hidden sea,
Murmurs of the moonlight, inviting us free.

In shadows we gather, where thoughts intertwine,
The dance of creation, so tender, so fine.
Every soft murmur a brush with the night,
In the moonlit embrace, we find our true sight.

Explore the vast silence, where wonders unwind,
In the echoes of moonlight, a glimpse of the mind.
With whispers of dreams, we learn to believe,
Murmurs of the night beckon us to weave.

The Unheard Symphony

In shadows deep, music brews,
Whispers dance on the night's hues.
Notes of longing, soft and sweet,
Echoes where heart and silence meet.

Strings of fate gently entwined,
Melodies lost, yet undefined.
Harmonies slide through the breeze,
A song forgotten, heart's unease.

Nature hums a quiet tune,
Stars above like notes in June.
Time may fade, yet they remain,
In every heart, a hidden pain.

The wind carries tales untold,
Of dreams in light and shadows bold.
Each sigh a note, each breath a chord,
The symphony neither heard nor stored.

In silence, beauty finds its voice,
In night's embrace, hear the choice.
Let go the din of day and strive,
To find the song that keeps us alive.

Threads of Tranquility

In the hush of dawn's first light,
Gentle breezes take their flight.
Nature whispers, soft and low,
A tapestry of peace to sow.

Golden rays weave through the trees,
Filling hearts with calming ease.
Every rustle, every sound,
Threads of tranquility abound.

Rippling streams, they softly flow,
Crystals glimmer in the glow.
Nature's brush paints life anew,
Colors blend in every view.

Mountains stand in quiet grace,
Guardians of this sacred space.
In their shadows, spirits lift,
As peace and wonder find their gift.

Underneath the vast sky's dome,
Hearts find refuge, rest, and home.
In moments still, the world feels right,
Threads of tranquility take flight.

Dreams Beyond the Veil

Softly drifting through the night,
Veils of dusk obscure the light.
Whispers call from realms unseen,
Where hopes and visions softly glean.

In twilight's embrace, we all find,
Starlit dreams that gently bind.
Fleeting shadows, dancing free,
Echoes of what's meant to be.

Time suspends in silent bliss,
Every heartbeat, every kiss.
Across the void, connections weave,
In dreams, we dare, we love, believe.

Secrets linger in the air,
Revealing truths, beyond compare.
Awakened souls, in silence soar,
On wings of visions, forevermore.

Beyond the veil, we feel the spark,
Where light ignites, erasing dark.
In dreams, we chase what lies ahead,
Alive in visions, not just read.

A Chorus of Forgotten Voices

In the echoes of the past,
Whispers fade, shadows cast.
Memories linger, soft and frail,
A chorus rises, lost in the gale.

What tales lie in silence held?
Each heartbeat, every life dispelled.
Voices merge, in twilight's glow,
Stories yearning to overflow.

In the ruins, ghosts take flight,
Paneling the canvas of night.
From the depths, the chorus sings,
Of lost hopes and forgotten things.

A bridge between what was and is,
Time weaves memories like a whiz.
In every note, we find reprieve,
A legacy that won't deceive.

Through the hum of life's embrace,
Echoes find a sacred place.
Let us listen, heed the sound,
In forgotten voices, wisdom found.

Whispers of a Forgotten Night

In shadows deep, where silence sways,
A tale unfolds in twilight's haze.
The breeze it tells, of dreams long lost,
Of whispered wishes, at any cost.

Moonbeams dance on leaves of gray,
Carrying secrets of yesterday.
Each rustling sound, a ghostly sigh,
In the quiet, the echoes lie.

Stars above, like candles burn,
Guarding the stories, we yearn to learn.
In the stillness, hearts collide,
With memories that time can't hide.

Forgotten hopes in shadows creep,
In the night's embrace, they gently weep.
A harmony of lost delight,
Whispers soft, in the still of night.

A fleeting moment, fleeting breath,
A reminder of the dance with death.
Yet in despair, there blooms a light,
In whispers of a forgotten night.

Echoes Beneath the Stars

Beneath the canvas of the night,
Stars whisper dreams, a soft delight.
With every twinkle, stories flow,
Of ancient love, and long ago.

Galaxies hum in fragile light,
As shadows play, and hearts ignite.
Each pulse of time, a tale retold,
In the tapestry of dreams, we hold.

A gentle breeze carries the song,
Of cosmic threads, where we belong.
The night surrounds, a velvet sea,
Echoes of what we long to be.

With every breath, our hopes take flight,
In the embrace of starry night.
Connections draw us ever near,
As whispers turn to laughter dear.

So gaze upon the vast expanse,
Join in the universe's dance.
With every echo, hearts will soar,
Beneath the stars, forevermore.

Murmurs in the Moonlight

Moonlit whispers on the ground,
With every step, a haunting sound.
In silver rays, the shadows play,
Murmurs of night, come what may.

The garden breathes a fragrant sigh,
As secrets flutter, and dreams fly high.
Among the blooms, the truth unfolds,
In soft tones, the night beholds.

Laughter echoes, faint but clear,
In the hush of night, so near.
Each flicker of light tells a tale,
Of love's journey, of hearts that sail.

In every sigh, the universe spins,
With hidden paths and timeless sins.
Murmurs weave through the starlit air,
Caressing souls who dare to care.

When dawn arrives, the whispers fade,
But in the heart, their charms are laid.
For every moment, a story bright,
Lives on in murmurs, in the moonlight.

Secrets of a Slumbering Soul

In the quiet of the fading day,
Secrets linger, lost in play.
A soul that dreams, so deep, so wide,
Hides the wonders it can't confide.

Echoes whisper tales of old,
In slumber's grip, the heart turns bold.
With every breath, a world awakes,
In silken threads, the slumber shakes.

Wandering thoughts, like drifting clouds,
Taking flight, beneath night shrouds.
A soft caress of starry glow,
Revealing secrets, hidden below.

Each dream a key, to worlds unknown,
In the lull of night, where kindness is sown.
From shadows rise, the light unfolds,
Unlocking tales, the moon beholds.

And when the sun begins to peep,
The secrets fade, but cannot keep.
For in the heart of a slumbering soul,
Lies a treasure, making us whole.

Still Waters Run Deep

In hushed tones, the river flows,
Reflecting skies, where calmness grows.
Beneath the surface, secrets lie,
Mysteries held, as time flows by.

Ripples dance with gentle grace,
Whispers of dreams in this sacred space.
A mirror to the stars above,
In stillness, find the strength of love.

Mountains cradle silent streams,
Nature cradles our deepest dreams.
A tranquil heart, an open mind,
In quiet depths, true peace we find.

Like shadows stretched at break of dawn,
Still waters cradle what is drawn.
Unseen currents weave through time,
A soothing pulse, a silent rhyme.

In every drop, a tale untold,
Life's ebbs and flows, both young and old.
Still waters sing a soft refrain,
In their embrace, our hearts remain.

Emotions Wrapped in Silence

A fluttered breath, a fleeting glance,
In silence blooms a quiet dance.
Words unspoken, yet understood,
In tender hush, raw feelings stood.

Behind closed doors, emotions swell,
In the depths, where shadows dwell.
A symphony of hearts in still,
Where absence echoes, time stands still.

Hands brush lightly, sparks ignite,
In every pause, the world takes flight.
Silence wraps the fragile bond,
In unvoiced love, we become fond.

A glance can speak more than the loud,
In quietude, our hearts avowed.
An uncharted path, we take our time,
In whispered hope, our spirits climb.

A tapestry of thoughts entwined,
In whispered breaths, the heart is blind.
Drawn together, yet worlds apart,
In the stillness lies a beating heart.

The Veil of Nightfall

As daylight fades, the shadows creep,
The sky adorned in twilight's sweep.
Stars awaken, one by one,
Veiling secrets that come undone.

Moonlight bathes the world in dreams,
Softly glistening like silver streams.
Night whispers tales of ages past,
In every breath, a spell is cast.

The hush of night holds mysteries vast,
In silent woods, where echoes last.
Beneath the stars, we seek and find,
In the veil of night, hearts entwined.

A shimmering cloak, the moonlight weaves,
With gentle hands, the world believes.
In the dark, the magic swells,
In quiet corners, the heart compels.

Embrace the shadows, let them ignite,
In the depth of night, we take flight.
Boundless dreams on silver beams,
The veil of night holds whispered dreams.

Beauty in the Quiet

In stillness blooms a gentle art,
Whispers cradle the beating heart.
A sunset's glow, a leaf's soft fall,
In quiet moments, there's beauty for all.

The soft rustle of the trees,
Stories shared upon the breeze.
In the silence, colors blend,
Nature's palette, without an end.

A soft sigh escapes the lips,
As sunlight on the water dips.
In tranquil spaces, peace unfolds,
A timeless tale, in silence told.

The world pauses, holds its breath,
In quietude, we dance with death.
Moments linger, pure and bright,
In the calm, we find our light.

The beauty lies in what we feel,
In whispered love, the heart can heal.
In every pause, each gentle glance,
Beauty thrives in the stillness' dance.

Shadows of Forgotten Aspirations

In whispers lost to time's own hands,
The dreams we had, like slipping sands.
Faded echoes in the dark,
Hopes once bright, now just a spark.

Chasing visions in the night,
Fleeting glances, lost in flight.
Once we soared on wings so high,
Now we linger, asking why.

Shadows dance on empty halls,
Silent echoes of our calls.
What if paths we never tread,
Held the words we never said?

But in the stillness, hearts can yearn,
A flickering flame, a chance to burn.
To grasp the stars we let slip by,
And paint our dreams across the sky.

So let us rise from ashes gray,
Rekindle hope in the light of day.
For shadows may obscure the light,
But in our hearts, the dreams ignite.

Gentle Night's Embrace

Softly falls the velvet night,
Whispers tender, bathed in light.
The world beneath a silver hue,
As stars awaken, one by two.

Crickets sing their lullabies,
While moonlight dances in the skies.
Wrapped in dreams and quiet peace,
Nighttime's magic grants release.

Shadows blend with dreams anew,
In this realm where wishes brew.
Every sigh a secret shared,
In gentle moments, hearts laid bare.

Twinkling gems of distant lore,
Call us to remember more.
Each heartbeat soft, a tender sigh,
In the night, we learn to fly.

Embrace the peace the stars provide,
In their glow, our fears subside.
With every breath, let hope ignite,
As we wander through the night.

Hushed Reveries

In the stillness, thoughts take flight,
Whispers of dreams bathed in light.
Moments linger, softly fade,
In the hush where hopes are made.

Silent echoes of desires pure,
Carved in shadows, paths obscure.
In memories, we find our truth,
Unraveling threads of fleeting youth.

Beneath the stars, we silently yearn,
For time's embrace, our hearts discern.
Longing glimpses, a fleeting touch,
In quiet corners that mean so much.

Every sigh a tale retold,
In secret realms where dreams unfold.
The heart's canvas, painted slow,
In hushed reveries, love shall grow.

So let us dwell where silence sings,
In the beauty that stillness brings.
For in the calm, our souls unite,
In the hushed glow of soft moonlight.

The Space Between Thoughts

In the silence, a breath is drawn,
A space where dusk meets dawn.
Thoughts collide, then drift away,
In the pause of night and day.

Moments hang like fragile threads,
Weaving dreams upon our beds.
In quiet corners, truth can gleam,
In the stillness, we can dream.

What lies in the spaces unseen,
Between the words, a world serene.
Fleeting shadows lightly brush,
In the gaps, hopes softly hush.

Here, the mind can wander free,
Between the notes of memory.
As echoes dance, thoughts intertwine,
In the silence, stars align.

So linger here, embrace the void,
In the silence, fears destroyed.
For in the quiet, truth reveals,
The space between is where it heals.

www.ingramcontent.com/pod-product-compliance
Ingram Content Group UK Ltd.
Pitfield, Milton Keynes, MK11 3LW, UK
UKHW030859221224
452712UK00007B/1064

9 789908 146485